A BELL OR A HOOK

A BELL OR A HOOK

Peter Fortunato

Ithaca House

1977

Some of these poems first appeared in *Epoch* and
Kuksu. Acknowledgement is made to the editors.

Copyright 1977, by Ithaca House

ITHACA HOUSE
108 North Plain St.
Ithaca, New York 14850

Ithaca House books are distributed by Serendipity
Books Distribution, 1790 Shattuck Ave., Berkeley,
CA 94709. Please place orders through them.

Library of Congress Cataloging in Publication Data

Fortunato, Peter, 1950-
    A bell or a hook.

    Poems.
    I.   Title.
PS3556.O753B4   811'.5'4   77-22186
ISBN 0-87886-087-8

for the Lady

CONTENTS

"What is there higher in this world
than the northern horn of the waning moon?
What is there lower in this world
than the southern horn of the waning moon?"

Looking back that trail
no-trail we took
just followed
map in hand
the signs,
the flowers:
spirea, labrador tea, false solomon's seal;
mountain heather was
"a gorgeous little evergreen
with purple cups on top"
I found
September 6 was
when I opened
to the wind
a puff-ball with some words;
"Go spores,
     one or two of you
        may take"

A bell or a hook
and it's hidden
— is the moon
out tonight?
There's the Bull and Orion;
now they're gone,
in the summer.
You are on
— I keep time.
You're a garden,
you, the plants
in the shade.
Too much sun.
I can't stop.
Then it's night
or you move
like the stars;
Witching steps,
white-water and falls.
I'm the hunter,
you're the game
we play.

    Those boots Mary wore
up the trail
            to the buttes
and today when we walked
back from Chuck's:
    "Sure are good
on these rocks, hold the path
with your feet"

                let a bear chase you
down, never up
and he falls cause his legs
    are too long in behind

    I dreamt Bob Greensfelder
came from the woods,
hair bristling, wild-eyed, said that he'd seen
Lew Welch: "He was different from us"
    or Albert Saijo dreamt the same thing.
Chuck told us his dream
of the tribe. It was Joel who was changed.

I dream that I change.
    And this shirt, emerald,
cut in the arc of the sun

satsang, sangha, we
dance in the whorl of our words, Gary said,
        and the grain is in us

        who you meet on the path,

who you are
where you turn when
        you're called
                        by the well at the source

        working down to
the stream
in the stone

I sleep aware of how
    I curl in bed —
  my knees drawn up
  behind, inside of hers
        curved;
    tucked foetally, spooned
against the smooth wide hips.

    how it is one body
that I share:
A mother's only child,
only man.

I am another growing
toward the pure, far sun
  out of rocks and dirt
and into other skins.

While the mid-afternoon sun
was ripe
    — first time I'd ever seen
    a hummingbird
                stop like that

in the branches of a pine —

We had to put ourselves
back to this:
                gold in the garden,
        straw mulch,

— and urine scent —
        how green
        how green

is the sea in the back
of the mind?

The sweat as it trickles,
all salt.

first oak leaves down
   yellow; poison-oak grows
crisp, red

            "red-off" bolitas mushroom
underside — golden pores means edible.
we had two — this early rain
                this september

and clouds three days
feathered whisk,
   faint froth above
      tall green ponderosa pine.
cool breeze
      like autumn; first time
for us
in california

      the east begins to fade.
"The sky is getting awfully blue."

"It's just all the different colors,
I think."

FOR THE SEED

8

          only as the passage of rain,
              it is known partly
in rain falling
on the quince and hawthorn,
apple and pear—

              fruit fallen
lies open, over-ripe
when october passes
              green again
into the night.

      I know
the whole motion
of this moment—
    Feeling,
having heard the drip
from house eaves onto

          an overturned metal pail
      sounding
              rain,

all the world is falling
whole
          and opens
for the seed.

SIERRA BODY, BREEZY DAY

Cloud body, rolling body
        of the earth.   Light pouring
    down through windy
crested pine nodding, bowing;
balanced globes of needles, clusters,
                                shine —
    and a cloud that shades my face.

I thought of all
    I thought blown down,
dissolving, turning,
            rising with this breeze
    whose body visits mine
and cools this longing:

light and shade.

BEGINNING WHERE

            Forty steps up —
three bags of cement; poured slab.
three packs of shingles
                to the roof
            and countless boards for shelves.
A job that nobody likes: lifting
the face on a one-time bungalow.

I carry up, I hammer down
            beginning work
near finished by others
            who weren't all that good
—I find their margins often wide —
beginning where they end.

Around the terraces in hills,
the houses cropping out on cliffs
            and views all different:
Tamalpais' green peaks
the sunny days
                or bannered with the fog.

From a high scaffold, nailing soffits
looking down —
        an oak leaf flutters by —
    look out
to blonde soft hills,
        slow learning
new woods, the limit of my sight.

Marin, 4:x:75

ON BOARD

Night long snuffled cold under
sleeping bags piled on bunk
    — touch of the flu; germ, you are too
    present —
            Dreamt of snowy Eastern hills:
I was pushing little cars who got stuck.
Meantime here in Sausalito harbor
three men hammer clank and pump
    that little fart of an engine
        under flood-light
try and float the skow next berth
       and get it outta there.

Dawn, sitting, back straightens
    — mental wince at constant noise,
begrudge them our lost sleep —
Who are we gonna save?
    Last crescent moon bright hook
    high tide —
         a tough old tug appears
    to pull the hulk!
—They labor out gate three.

bright, bright yellow sun
empty water mirror sky

HE IS THE LORD of old wood
    and sheet-rock crumbling
from walls that I wreck
        with the blows of my hammer —
The Lord of the Dance —

Lord of Spiders
nesting in close dark spaces exposed:
    the skeleton of a forty year old house,
douglas fir
going rotten, full of bugs —
  a dynasty of termites dismantle
the frame — my work too; Yours,
SHIVA
        wielding the hammer,
pry-bar, screwdriver, and sledge —
STRIKE THRU MY ARM!

        shatter siding of redwood,
oak planks on the floor,
plaster-board,
cheap plywood veneer,
cast-iron pipes,
        tear out the porcelain fixtures now
useless for flushing down shit —

that we may rebuild,

    in our work be renewed

here on hills above
   an opulent little town
that sucks at the jewel of the Bay.

Dirty and worn, ragged
   by the end of each day —
house coming down bit by bit
going home.
"even a broken diamond
is more precious than gold"

Sausalito, 18:X:75

I felt the sun move
        by the shadow
    cast from a windows corner.
The boat lists, moored;
everything slips out of place.

        Sunday, docks full
of noise:
            'When you live in the ways,
when you live in the ways...'
Hammers and engines come on.

Shelter, food, some source
        of heat — kerosene furnace or
a small wood-stove —
        raise a little smoke.
Nights the peninsula blinks
in and out of the fog:
                    Bay window

LOVE SONG

16

rain running
     down the length of tarred roof
  boat leaking in on us:

hiss on the wood-stove
and water ran down
     through a window sash
        beside our bed.

sheets of rain thrown back
above our heads.
    We heard the wind
       slapping slack lines
      against the masts
the tick of time

before, and again after

FIRST THOUGHT; NO THOT

just today reflected, working
        doing my job
just this:

        hanging floor joists of douglas fir, 2 x 8
        butting four-by beams;
        and set with sixteen-penny nails

this will last

        some things I wanted, spoke to others,
called myself in dream and meant to grab
disappear
                in the low slant of sun's
                late autumn light

my words

        and I heard Dylan's voice
cresting, breaking thru waves of radio
boldly accusative "story of the Hurricane"
roaring that "Ruben Carter was falsely tried"

before the millions

I pause, idle a moment
hammer dangles in my hand

headlands pressing out
    into a sea of buckled serpentine;
cloud on cloud
    against the thin bright trail
  the laser cuts
for time: behind the golden gate,
    ash grey sky

How many nails I bent, couldn't
hammer; You hit your finger
    how many times?

Felt worthless, all I managed
was one form that, empty,
    would shape walls of poured concrete.

    and bruised my knee somehow;
I pricked my thumb on something sharp
— bled through grime and sucked it clean —
slipped, banging my back
last thing today as I was leaving the job.

It was raining there at four;
not a decent shred of work all day.
Gave up, got paid anyhow.

When I got back, wet, cold
and tied inside with thick coarse rope
I wept in rage it was just frustration
— she said she'd felt that way before.

hot food and drunk
made love
    — too greedy

this is your koan;
breathing my lover's chestnut hair.

WHAT IS IT BUT

silken smoke helix
    slowly burning cigarette;

home, flu
remedies: 'give him some coffee
      and leave him alone'
(north beach italians)

plover in the mudflat —
catch his call

    cassette music, blue

rain whipping my cheek, drips
on my neck —
              the slick wet planks of
scaffolding three stories high
I quit for home.

"and that's the deal" Pete our neighbor said
at dockside: he surveys his stack of
drenched cold lumber; nods and frowns.
              Wind whining thru masts
        and boats must sway or slip at pilings
        squeeking collared rubber tires.
Clamor heard from steel framed hull where
some are working
                      eight months now.

A congress of gulls wheels
in at port; scavenger full time occupies
        george washington holiday
I observe —
                to the work alone are you entitled.

16:II:76

ALEMBIC (THE WORK)

> "But if you have no faith?
> In that case have a fire —
> that is all the alchemy is"

Where am I making fire — I was numb —
    still dark, I wanted
    light between my eyes.
The first step out is dawn;

then the stones, and mud
and trees: Alchemy is like gardening
like fishing
for the moon in water
                scalloped by the wind.

    The storm, a southerly, blew in
our harbor, hailed our ship
and rocking,
    rocking — night or day — the dream:
Our atoms, seconds, turn the distant nebulae.
We touch the stars at dusk.

I saw it all as fire
lit the windows in the hills
    across the harbor;
                    clear sky, cut glass
glowing alpine rose
reflected polar flashing light
        and birds who break the surface
                    after fish:
        all my art
is mirror, as the moon

Two hammers falling thru fog
this morning:
          steel workers ringing
the ribs of a ship.

The cold snaps and acacia blossoms.

Each poem is written,
  each picture fades
and the world floats thru the past
            with its bell.

little devils armed with tridents
poking the sleeper awake
    — little rascals

    me and my fork
turning the dirt
picking it up:
            manure means shit!

It's the Garden,
it's 'Hell on Earth'
it's the fire inside
            makes things grow.

tilling four beds at a time,
sowing seeds
reaping poems

— and that's the way it works.

THREADS

lighter than air, climbing
the breeze: shine
silk drifts by
bearing new green worm-bodies
curled like fiddleneck fern
flexing
from pines
out of doors
where I pass;

tangle my hair
clinging, crossing my eyes
and barely there

cobwebs catching light
caught me, dry catkins, all
hung up under oak.

cross-cutting boards and boards and boards;
ripping them down, smaller
     into dust; you breathe it,
   it's everywhere
   — finally gone, too
into earth.

— what you think you saw —

a thousand petals crowning it all,
the shadows lacing with the path.

The sun was a mare, a palomino.
Moon was my horse I was afraid
she hadn't been stabled. We were
walking past the place
where the old barn used to stand it
was there again and I said
I had to check to see
if the horses were alright.
I called the Sun and she
was there, a nicker;
saw her big gold rump,
she cocked her hind foot and
the steel shoe gleamed.
This was at night. I looked for Moon.
Her stall was pitched
behind a black hay mow.
It was dark in there and suddenly
she moved up close to me
seal-brown and
out of the darkness too.

Water the garden;
When the earth is softened,
plant —
         the seeds for gourds,
cut
      the grass for mulch.

And pull weeds
along the gravel band
that borders on the house

— this to break a fire
should it happen,
when it comes —

Practice your dance.

You were a little girl
whose long thin legs
            they called 'totem poles'
— and the crone in my dream:
Your stockings wrinkled, brown,
        rolled to your knees;
At a bus stop in the snow
                from behind.

    Your warm places —
I touch you there.
            hot sun, a heavy humid breeze
                at the shore.

or fucking on a high bed;
Grecian,
        Queen of the Glades.
flash of your teeth, nape, thighs;
and your limbs —
    all the boughs that I bend.

in the many,
     the one wheel
all the spokes, humming
      rays of light
— bugs in a swirl
  on the rim
  of a world

Maya, your cup
at my lips
  calochortus, today
  'beautiful grass'
wherever I looked;
Stunned with the passage
of time, Mother

  one year ago

  trout-lilies
bursting from the flow.

Before me
parting
          forest mist and
    from behind that
lifted sleeping
figures; trees sway
              voluptous
        women, yakshi, deva —
Moons all setting full

Still dark;
arms raised, thighs white
                  separate,
open slitted gowns
to the hip: Dancing, hold me
while it lights
        so close, as fine
as froth
          rising
bodies slight as sighs —
that silk caress the skin
awake

Earth moving
    Wind
            moving me,
            parting

offered life, who
    offered
herself, I am loved
and loving see myself
    in her departing, woman-wise
  to other men.

She gave me voice —
Praise green crests and gorges,
    body of the Yuba.
  sunset from porch of study-hut
cross-legged over woven rug
blue and gold and red
                crossed dorje.
Colors primary in the mind —
    mauve and delicate orange
    over west.
Quick green flame spreading
under sky now vague
and rolling back from blue
    as light grows lean spectral band.

And she without me,
    within,
            has gone sure steps down path
through woods of pine and oak
    and manzanita brush,
— same woods I look down through
perched on granite in the hills —
        to find a place
        her own
                (my lady of the waters,
watch you wading in the green sun
that shines up through the river bed;
you roll your hips
and beckon
            near some rocks, knee-deep in sparkling
Yuba light —
            I watch you still
tonight from where I sift the dusk for gold)
Enchanting you as well,
    I wander my own trail up to this height.

34

BOM BOM MAHA DEV!

           ringing down ridge
voiced the shape
of wings;
           Crickets sing inside the moon
           that waits to rise behind the sun.
Lighting lantern, twilit sky
I think of you, loving
      loved —
Myself in you, woman-flesh,
   breath and heat
and swift wet flow;
      my lady in the stream,
I offer all I can:
                  my tangled early thoughts
      possessive of your love —
I give them up. Your own ways, too, I leave off
                                    here.
      Night spent in recollection;
poring over dark waving hills —
moth wing, bat wing
                  steady flicking through air —
      My lover off, down clear woods trail

"It started at the top of the hill by Dovey's
and knocked three trees down across their lawn,
then it split (the wind) itself in two —
went on the side of the kitchen split the tree
        by the dining room in two,
knocked down all the trees on that side,
knocked down Dovey's trees where I had
        the clothesline,
knocked down all the apple trees behind the pool
(when I say knocked down I mean uprooted)
on the side of the car-port it knocked down
        the first four trees,
the other three had to be cut because they were
        leaning over,
the first four trees fell across Roy's driveway
        toward his lawn
and then the two big trees on Roy's lawn
        went down —
bringing the light pole down with it, one tree
        hit the edge of Roy's house
damaging his chimney and antenna —

to top it all the temperature dropped that night —
Monday morning woke up freezing —
luckily around ten o'clock in the morning
        a crew came
and started working,
when I got home at night
the power was on.

''Myself I have been on the verge of tears
since Sunday afternoon.''

THE LOTUS, JEWELLED,
REFLECTED IN

the rooms of sun all the rooms of
light, trapped exploding entire
worlds in worlds the germ of living flame
unfolding petals blossoms in
the husk of life, a cradle
for the seed:

where small ponds, canyons,
cups of water drawn into the tracks
of an old mare crossing a wet swale
beside the burning scar
nods her head, swarms of flies
revolve about her only life:

each life is held, holds its own sharp
moment cut into a form
ten thousand ways of seeing
one blooded rose.

Kicked down a sandy road
and made my way
        along a ridge;   songbirds,
gravel crunch, the creak of rocking wood
in the breeze.
Dark windy sky,
buffed clouds and the sun-shaft
        down through a crack
in the shell —
We are in the world.
    pale green willows, white pine,
young maples
enter rain.

Bleeding from the head,
        hair matted and
    the blood clot
    stiff; hair growing silent
out of bodies silent already
            in the ground.
Fresh corpses waking,
        loose ends
    dangling tiny skulls.
The hair of death
is rank with snakes
    and ties
            the mortal knot.

— This pain and rage
leaks down my limbs
        all cracked
and shakes me, rattling
        fear
long death coming day;
itch, my only hide
for worms:

        O, lizard blooming rose
salamander of flame
        scarlet dappled ember
    Breathing-Skin
come forth!
            Thunder-Lizard
    knock my bones awake,
first father
may I enter your samadhi
— fire is your place —
unborn, resume
this trembling earth
        our circle is complete.

Sometimes it makes you want
        to go back to sleep,
    and there's a lull —
Those breakers, a memory
complete.

But the sky slips blue into a body
of blue water
        and it's deafening: the moon
        rattling her hooves in a cup:

There's an ocean
raises it's head,
        foam in the crest
        of each wave

for Chuck

        given that work
you obey: turn your mind
            at the lathe
and marry your hands
to the craft.
    A wife is silver,
    a child is gold;
Where could the Pearl
have been hidden —
        Count the moons and the suns;
String the bead in each day
with a scarlet thread.
Prick the stones for their blood,
give it back.
        Crown each death
with the birth of new light
in your eye.

OM AH HUM
VAJRA GURU PADME SIDDHI HUM

I draw serpent ridges
        north of us
    in clouds, a dragon arching

clear dry hills.

Meadows of weeds loose mice
and cats;
            my legs are scratched and bare.
We have ourselves a drought,
a waxing moon, low tides.

    In a vision Tamalpais'
wreath of wealth;
Bald Mountain struck with rain.
The music on and on
                so many moons
a round of frozen smoke.

Each lord of thot
        each sees the whole
    moving
his world.
Thunder and Rain,
        what do they say?
...all you know,
all that you want...
The Flood and Tide
making over the Earth
        every day
    nothing in mind.

A Bell or a Hook was handset in Perpetua type and
letterpress printed on Warren's Olde Style
laid paper by Peter Fortunato,
Barbara Siegel, and Joe Freedman.
Design by Barbara Siegel and
linocut by Barbara Larsen